No Pressure,
Mr. President!

OTHER BOOKS BY ERIC METAXAS

Bonhoeffer: Pastor, Martyr, Prophet, Spy

*Amazing Grace: William Wilberforce and
the Heroic Campaign to End Slavery*

*Socrates in the City: Conversations on "Life,
God, and Other Small Topics"*

*Everything You Always Wanted to Know
About God (but Were Afraid to Ask)*

*Everything Else You Always Wanted to Know
About God (but Were Afraid to Ask)*

*Everything You Always Wanted to Know About God
(but Were Afraid to Ask): The Jesus Edition*

No Pressure, Mr. President!

The Power of True Belief in a Time of Crisis

ERIC METAXAS

Thomas Nelson
Since 1798

NASHVILLE   DALLAS   MEXICO CITY   RIO DE JANEIRO

Published in Nashville, Tennessee, by Thomas Nelson. Thomas Nelson is a registered trademark of Thomas Nelson, Inc.

Thomas Nelson, Inc., titles may be purchased in bulk for educational, business, fund-raising, or sales promotional use. For information, please e-mail SpecialMarkets@ThomasNelson.com.

Photos used by permission of Rick Potter of Potter Photo Studios. Video used by permission of The National Prayer Breakfast.

Scripture noted KJV is from the King James Version.

ISBN: 978-1-4002-7601-1
ISBN: 978-1-4002-7502-1 (e-book)

Printed in the United States
12 13 14 15 16 TSB 6 5 4 3 2 1

CONTENTS

CHAPTER 1

A Funny Thing Happened on the Way to the
National Prayer Breakfast

1

CHAPTER 2

The National Prayer Breakfast Address

31

CHAPTER 3

Can I Get a Picture?

55

Watch the Address

61

About the Author

62

I think this is where I claimed that **Tony Bennett** had written the eighteenth-century hymn **"Amazing Grace."** As it happens, he didn't. My only real goal that morning was to be **taller** and **funnier** than **Mother Teresa.** Of course, history will be the judge on that score.

With appreciation to Rick Potter of Potter Photo Studios for permission to use

1

A FUNNY THING
HAPPENED ON THE
WAY TO THE NATIONAL
PRAYER BREAKFAST

don't know about you, but in my life thus far, I haven't often had the opportunity to speak in front of the president of the United States. Or to chit-chat with the vice president or to publicly pretend the former Speaker of the House is my wife or to lead thirty-five hundred people in singing "Amazing Grace." A capella. But unless I dreamed it, I did have the opportunity to do all these things once. It was at something called the National Prayer Breakfast. It was an extraordinary experience and I'd love to tell you about it. But maybe I should back up a bit.

The first time I ever got a hint that I might be involved in the National Prayer Breakfast was in a barbershop in Manhattan.

I was waiting for my barber—yes, his name is Angelo—to finish with the person ahead of me when my cell phone rang. It was Foncie Bullard, a friend of mine from Fairhope, Alabama. Foncie told me that she had just spoken with Alabama senator Jeff Sessions about the possibility of my appearing at a prayer breakfast. At least that's what I heard. I had spoken at the Louisiana Governor's Prayer Breakfast in 2008, as the guest of Governor Bobby Jindal, so the prospect of speaking at the Alabama Prayer Breakfast seemed perfectly plausible. I do a lot of public speaking, and I hoped that eventually someone in another state would contact me about speaking at another prayer breakfast. I would love to go back to Alabama to see my friends there. I'd spoken in Mobile, Alabama, several times and in Birmingham, Alabama, twice. I'd even spoken in Marion, Alabama, at Judson College.

But Foncie didn't seem to think that I was as impressed as I should be. "You don't seem that excited," she said.

I didn't know what she expected. I said, "I'm excited and grateful to be asked, of course! I guess I'm just not as surprised as I would be if I had never spoken at a prayer breakfast before."

Foncie paused. "But this is the *National* Prayer Breakfast," she said.

The National Prayer Breakfast? Had I heard that right? I had. Well, naturally that was something else entirely. "Oh," I said, feeling not a little stupid for having missed this. The noise in the barbershop was part of the reason. But what I understood still wasn't all that clear. I thought Foncie was saying that in the next few days I *might* be invited by Alabama senator Jeff Sessions to be a *part* of the National Prayer Breakfast in Washington, DC. In some capacity. I knew that I would *not* be asked to be the keynote speaker. That was out of the question, and it never even crossed my mind. But perhaps I would be asked to read a Scripture or something.

The keynote speaking slot was a position reserved for heads of state, or for someone *like* a head of state, someone like Mother Teresa, like Tony Blair, or Bono. At least those were the three big names that came to mind whenever I thought of the National Prayer Breakfast. They had been keynote speakers, as had many other luminaries. So I knew I wasn't being asked to be the keynote speaker. But the very idea that I might be invited to take part in any capacity was a huge honor, and I looked forward to hearing from Senator Sessions.

I wondered what role they might ask me to play. Perhaps I would be invited to give a short speech, like the one my New York firefighter friend Joe Finley had given in 2002. Joe had been one of the firefighters at the World Trade Center the day the towers came down. My dear friend B. J. Weber—who actually was connected with the Fellowship, the folks who put on the prayer breakfast—had befriended Joe and suggested that he speak at the breakfast. So at the breakfast in 2002, Joe gave a short speech of five or six minutes, recounting his experiences on that terrible and memorable day.

Whatever role I would play, the thought of being involved in any way was humbling and exciting. I might even get to meet the president. Not to mention the keynote speaker! Whoever that might be. Wait—maybe it would be Tim Tebow! The previous year it had been the film director Randall Wallace, who wrote *Braveheart* and directed *Secretariat*. They never told you who the keynote speaker was ahead of time. But it really could be anyone. Still, I tried not to get too excited about any of it, because these inquiries—Foncie's phone call, for example—were usually just tentative feelers and might actually mean nothing. I recalled that when George Pataki was governor, I had been told over the phone that I was chosen to speak at the New York State Prayer Breakfast in Albany, only to have the invitation mysteriously rescinded a few weeks later. I'd rather not get my hopes up to have them dashed. So I took on a stoic attitude.

Later that day, I thought more about the National Prayer Breakfast. The first time I had ever heard about it was through B. J. Weber, whom I mentioned, and my friend Jim Lane. I came to know Jim in 1994, when I was living in New Canaan, Connecticut. He and I started a men's Bible study that met in his living room that year, which in the years since has grown and grown into something called the New Canaan Society. Jim and B. J. would go to the National Prayer Breakfast almost every year, but I hardly knew what it was. Then, in 1997, thanks to the two of them, I went too.

And who could forget *that* prayer breakfast?

It took place just two weeks after the Lewinsky scandal broke—like a rotten egg—all over the culture. Of course that hadn't been planned. On the contrary, it must have been a nightmare for the president and for the people putting on the prayer breakfast. The tradition was that the president *always* appeared at this event and spoke. So I remember thinking that the very idea of President Clinton walking into a room filled with Christian conservatives was the proverbial nonstarter. I refused to believe he would show up. Somehow he just had to find a way to wriggle out of this extremely awkward obligation. I had a seat near the very back of the room, which is so vast that the people on the dais in the distance seem like ants. But then in walked Bill Clinton—or at least that's who I assumed it was, since everyone stood and the band played "Hail to the Chief" as a tiny figure crossed the stage and took its position near the center of the long dais.

As he strode into the vast room there was an odd—indeed a unique—sound, like thousands of tinkling glasses. Technically it was applause, since it consisted of people putting their hands together again and again. But it was only *technically* applause, because it was very different from actual applause. It had to be the most restrained applause in the history of clapping. It was a homeopathic tincture of applause, an applause that flirted with the very definition of the word—that seemed to tease it and make sport of it. The people in the room had a tremendous respect for the office of the presidency, but because of this they also had a palpably negative feeling for the man entering the room, whose boisterous shenanigans had in the past weeks been ubiquitously examined and discussed. And so the superlatively strange tinkling sound that I heard that morning I surmised to be the sound of thirty-five hundred people applauding the *office* of the presidency. Applauding only that, and nothing more. One might listen for several lifetimes and listen in vain for that baffling, that tragic, sound.

The only other time I had attended the National Prayer Breakfast was in 2002. The president at that time was George W. Bush and, of course, only months earlier the nation had suffered the monstrous tragedy of the 9/11 attacks. Up on the dais that day was Lisa Beamer, the widow of Todd Beamer, who had used the phrase "Let's roll" as he heroically led his fellow passengers in an attempt to take down the plane before it could hit its target, which was the US Capitol building. Todd Beamer had been a Wheaton College graduate, as was my friend Jim Lane, who had invited me that morning. Also on the dais was the Speaker of the House, Denny Hastert, another Wheaton alumnus.

And finally, there on the dais was my new friend, New York City firefighter Joe Finley, whom I've mentioned. Since I am a writer, B. J. Weber, who had arranged for Joe to speak, asked me if I would mind helping Joe craft his speech. Of course I was honored to do so. Whether I had a hand in helping with it or not, it was a thrill to hear Joe tell his moving story that morning in front of all those people and the president of the United States.

These two events had been extraordinary and memorable. Nonetheless, I am not a morning person. So after the 2002 breakfast, I was pretty sure I wouldn't be returning for quite some time. The pressure to make conversation with strangers in that loud, vast room could be a bit much. And being seated something like a quarter of a mile from the people on the dais was also not my cup of tea. I figured that in the future I might attend some of the events surrounding the breakfast—for example, I had spoken at Cal Thomas's Media Dinner in 2011, which is always held on the night before the Prayer Breakfast, in the same hotel—but I certainly didn't plan on going back to the National Prayer Breakfast itself. And did I mention that it cost $175?

Of course the phone call in the barbershop would alter those plans.

In that phone call it really had sounded as if there was a decent chance that I would play some role in the upcoming National Prayer Breakfast. But as I said, I wasn't holding my breath. Then, lo and behold, the very next morning there it was: an e-mail from someone in Senator Sessions' office! It was from the senator's executive assistant, who told me that she would later that day be mailing the invitation for me to be the keynote speaker at the National Prayer Breakfast. But since regular mail could be slow, and because my calendar might be filling up, they had attached a scanned copy of the invitation letter with the e-mail, just so I would know right away.

But a strange thing happened when I read her e-mail. Somehow—please don't ask me for details—my eyes glossed over the word *keynote*. Perhaps we see what we want to see or what we expect to see, and I expected to read a letter inviting me to play a small role in the upcoming National Prayer Breakfast, not to be the keynote speaker.

I then opened the attachment to read the official invitation letter. It was from Senator Sessions and from Senator Mark Pryor of Arkansas. But in reading their letter I *again* glossed over the word *keynote*. I'm not making this up. As my addled mind read and reread the letter (you will recall that I am not a morning person), I eventually did see the word. And slowly it began to dawn on me that I may have misread the situation and that perhaps I was not being invited to be *one* of the speakers at the National Prayer Breakfast, but to be *the* speaker—to be the *keynote* speaker.

I wasn't prepared to absorb this information. I simply didn't know how to take it in. So I didn't take it in. I sort of hovered in the space above the words, unable to allow them to penetrate my brain. I assumed there was a mistake of some kind, and that if I read the letter carefully enough, I would see there was some crucial clause I had missed. But eventually I realized that there was nothing else to it. There was no missing clause. It was a stranger-than-fiction truth: I was being invited to be the keynote speaker at the National Prayer Breakfast.

At this point I needed a witness. "Susanne!" I called to my wife, not taking my eyes off the screen, lest the magic e-mail disappear and never return. "Would you come here, please?" Susanne came into the room and corroborated what I was reading. For some reason, it really did take time to sink in. I'm not sure what the mind is doing as something sinks in, nor what "sinks in" really means, but eventually I came to believe that this invitation was real, and not just a vain imagining on my part. The invitation was from one Republican senator (Sessions) and one Democratic senator (Pryor), as all National Prayer Breakfast invitations were, because the National Prayer Breakfast is all about setting aside partisan differences and "coming together in the Spirit of Jesus," as they invariably put it.

And so they had invited me to be the keynote speaker at the 60th Annual National Prayer Breakfast. There was only one downside to this fantastic news: I probably wouldn't be meeting Tim Tebow.

Later that morning the phone rang, and it was Senator Sessions' office, with the senator on the line. He called to ask me whether I would accept the invitation. Of course there was no question whether I would accept. But I couldn't just say yes. I had to play hard to get. So I asked whether the gig included breakfast. He laughed and said that it did. And then I decided to push it: Would they throw in breakfast for my wife and daughter? They would. Well, that was all it took.

Later in the day I fielded another call, this time from Senator Pryor. I was not used to getting phone calls from United States senators. I had once chatted with Senator Joe Lieberman and had once in an airport buttonholed Al Franken, whom people have said I resemble, presumably to nettle me. But to yak on the blower in my living room with senators from Alabama and Arkansas was something new.

In any case, I was told in the course of these phone calls that I mustn't broadcast the news of my being chosen. Certainly not to any media outlets. The National Prayer Breakfast had a strict policy of always keeping the keynote speaker secret. I knew I couldn't tell the media, but I was free to tell a few friends, and at the top of that list were my friends Jim Lane and B. J. Weber, whom I called immediately.

But now that all that was settled, and I really was to be the speaker, what would I talk about?

Of course, the opportunity to address the president of the United States and innumerable dignitaries from around the world could be—how does one put it—paralyzing. But by God's grace, it wasn't. I knew very well that the invitation was a miracle, so I really could trust God with the results. It followed logically that if Jesus had chosen me to speak—for his purposes—I could count on the fact that he had something to say, and that he wanted to say it more than I wanted him to say it. I could absolutely trust him with all of it, and I knew that, which was extraordinarily freeing. All I had to do was get out of the way, as they say. So I was very happily confident in him about the whole thing. I was absolutely sure that Jesus would take the wheel when I got behind the podium on the morning of the breakfast.

As the weeks passed I prayed about it. Now and again I had ideas and phrases I thought were worth jotting down. I often get ideas while running around the Central Park Reservoir. At some point during those weeks I remembered Mother Teresa's famous speech from 1994. I hadn't been there, but a number of my friends had—including Jim and B. J.—and people had been talking about it ever since. Mother Teresa had spoken of abortion as the greatest enemy of peace, because it is the taking of a life of the most innocent among us. And she had done so within a few feet of President and Mrs. Clinton, saying, "Don't kill your babies! Give them to me!" What she had said that day somehow inspired me. I could certainly not speak with the moral authority of this woman who was considered a living saint when she was still among us. But perhaps I, too, ought to say something about this incredibly important issue of innocent life. In any case, I had lots of ideas, as usual, and I wasn't used to writing out a completely new speech. In most of my speaking engagements I typically just tell the story of Bonhoeffer's life or the story of Wilberforce's life. But this was something unprecedented.

The invitation had come mid-November, so I had plenty of time to think about what I would eventually say. But Christmas came and went, and I still didn't have any clear sense of what I would be talking about. And as the New Year came, I realized I had many speaking engagements to keep me busy throughout January. And then, in the second half of January, I would have to go to Germany for a week. My Bonhoeffer book had been translated into German, and the Willow Creek Church pastor, Bill Hybels, had invited me to speak at a large conference he was putting on in Stuttgart. And just a few days after I got back from Germany, the big date would be here! Perhaps it was just about time to get cracking on what I was going to say, eh?

As I was packing for Germany, I took DVDs of some of the previous years' National Prayer Breakfast talks with me, hoping they would give me some help in what direction I might take. I'd intended to watch these DVDs for weeks, but I had been very busy. Now at last on my long flight to Germany, I would have time. And so, someplace above the clouds over the Atlantic, I watched them all. For some reason, however, they didn't help me figure out what I wanted to say.

But they did help me figure out what I would *wear*. Most of the people in the DVDs I watched were wearing business suits. I now resolved that instead of wearing a blue blazer as formerly planned, I would wear the only bespoke suit I owned: a double-breasted chalk pinstripe, created by that Michelangelo of the sartorial arts, Domenico Spano of New York City! "Mimmo," as he is known, had finished the suit just before I left for Germany, and I was scouring the landscape of my schedule book for an opportunity to wear it. My gaze settled on February 2 and the National Prayer Breakfast. The momentous question had been settled.

But what about the speech?

Alas, I still wasn't sure about that. Besides, I was so busy once I got to Europe, that I couldn't think much about it. First there was the business of getting over jet lag, and then there was a tour of downtown

Basel, and the next day there was a personal tour of Karl Barth's home in Basel. I even got to hold the letters that Dietrich Bonhoeffer had written to him. This was an extraordinary privilege. The next evening I spoke at a church, and the following day I spoke to a group of students at a beautiful old seminary called St. Chrischona, and then I hustled to the Zurich airport to catch a flight to Frankfurt, since I was speaking that evening at an event in Wiesbaden.* And the next morning I took the train down to Stuttgart! I had been extremely busy since I had landed, and not a moment had presented itself where I might cogently think about my speech.

But I sincerely knew it would all come together, that the Lord really was in charge of it all, as I have said. Besides, I now had formed a general idea of what I was going to say. I was going to tell the story of my coming to faith. But I didn't really need to write it down. I had told it so many times before and sometimes writing things down could kill the spontaneity.

But one afternoon while I was resting in my hotel room in Stuttgart, I got an e-mail from the folks who run the breakfast, asking me for a transcript of the talk. Er, transcript? No one had breathed a word about wanting a transcript in the nearly three months since the invitation. And now they said they needed it in the next day or so. I certainly didn't have any transcript, mainly because *I hadn't written it yet*. And as I have said, I wasn't planning to write it out. When I speak publicly, I speak from notes, usually written out on a single page. There simply was no transcript, I hadn't planned on creating

---

* There I met the sons of two of the heroes in my book on Bonhoeffer: Paul von Hase and Fabian von Schlabrendorf.

one, and now I was in Germany, exhausted from speaking many times and having to speak again two more times. What to do?

The folks in Washington said that because there would be more than a hundred countries represented in the room, the translators would need to have the transcript ahead of time, so they could prepare. I couldn't know if this was the real reason the folks asking for the transcript needed it or if it was just a ruse to get the speaker to volunteer his speech so they could vet it for length and content. After all, the president would be there. In any case, I now knew I would have to get them *something*. But when? I still had to appear with Bill Hybels in front of eight thousand people at the Porsche Stadium in Stuttgart, and then I had to speak at an evening event put on by my German publisher, SCM Haenssler. When would I have time to whip up a transcript of my speech? And then it struck me: I would turn to the task on the plane ride back.

During the plane ride home on Saturday, I tried to pull my notes together and begin tapping something out. I knew what I wanted to say, roughly, but for some reason I didn't seem to be able to write it down. As I neared the coast of North America with nothing written, I told myself that once I was back home in New York—in the bosom of my family—I would be able to type up the basics of what I had to say. The National Prayer Breakfast was four days away.

But when I got back home, there was once again the issue of jet lag. Not only that, I was exhausted from the extreme busyness of my trip and speaking so often and I just wasn't feeling very well. Whether it was jet lag or general fatigue I don't know, but even now at home I was having a very hard time writing anything. What could be done? As they say, you can't get blood from a stone. Or a turnip. Or since I was just back from Luther's Germany, *Einen Fortz von einem toten Mann.**

Finally on that Monday—a mere forty hours before we had to leave for DC—I managed to peck out the basic story of my coming to faith. This was what I had finally settled on, to tell the story of my coming to faith, which culminates in an extraordinary and life-changing dream that I had one night around my twenty-fifth birthday. At the heart of the dream is an image from a fairy tale— a golden fish. I've told the story so many times that many of my friends are probably tired of hearing it. They know it as the story of "The Golden Fish." I was planning to segue from that personal story to the basic difference between dead religion and real faith in Jesus.

The next day, Tuesday, I figured it was time to get another haircut. In case I haven't mentioned it, I would be meeting the president of the United States in two days. And the next day my wife and daughter and I would be flying down to DC at noon. Months before I had known I was going to be the speaker at the National Prayer Breakfast, I had been invited to be the keynote speaker at *another* event in DC the night before. It was for the Conference of Christian Colleges and Universities (CCCU) and it was in another Hilton, about a mile from the Capitol Hilton, where the National Prayer Breakfast was always held. It was hard not to marvel at the coincidence of this, if you believe in coincidences, which I don't. The idea that I was booked to speak the night before the prayer breakfast at a place one mile away was at least odd. But it was a fact. My wife and daughter and I needed

---

* "A flatus from a dead man."

to get to DC early that Wednesday so I could be rested to speak that evening—and then I would race back to our hotel and get to bed as early as possible in order to have enough time to wake up at 5:00 a.m. in advance of the super-early National Prayer Breakfast!

But this was still Tuesday morning and I was on my way to get a haircut in Manhattan. In case you were wondering, I get them regularly. The good news was that my talk was basically done. The bad news was that in the cab on the way to the barbershop, my phone rang. It was Jim Lane. He and his wife, Susie, were driving down from Vermont to Washington to be at the prayer breakfast. Jim wanted to touch base and see how I was doing. I told him I was fine—tired from the Germany trip, but basically fine—and that my talk was mostly done and I was on my way to get a haircut. He then asked what I was going to speak about. "Well," I said, "I'm basically going to give my testimony—the story of the dream—and then talk about the difference between faith and dead religion. But it's mainly the story of the dream."

"You mean 'Golden Pond'?" Jim said, unintentionally referring to the Henry Fonda–Katharine Hepburn movie from the eighties.

"Yeah," I said, knowing what he meant to say. "The Golden Fish. The story of the Golden Fish."

"Right, the Golden Fish." Jim paused. "Are you sure you want to tell that? It might not be right for this crowd—"

I knew Jim might say this. And as I took it in, I feared that he just might be right. This was indisputably grievous news. "I was thinking you'd talk about Bonhoeffer," he continued. "Isn't that probably what they're expecting? And maybe you would say a few words about Wilberforce? I think because of the success of the Bonhoeffer book that's probably what they would be looking for. I mean, it's your speech, but think about it."

I cringed, because I didn't want to think about it. Who would want to think about it, the day before leaving for DC? Who would want to consider the idea that the whole speech needed to be rewritten now, on the eve of my departure?

But as much as I hated to hear what Jim was saying, I was reasonably open to it, because I had a keen sense that Jesus would guide me in what to say, and it might well be that this was how he was guiding me—through my friend Jim. Stranger things have happened. So I told Jim I would think about it and pray about it, which I did.

After my haircut I went home and called B. J. Weber, to see what he thought. And let's face it, I hoped he would tell me he thought Jim was out of his gourd, and to just go ahead and tell the story of the Golden Fish, that it was *perfect* for this crowd. B. J. had been closely involved with the National Prayer Breakfast for decades and he would know what was best. But B. J. simply and flatly agreed with Jim's assessment. Let me be frank: this was unpleasant. But it was a fact, and as far as I was concerned, that was that. Two for two. And so—alas and alack—I had to agree that this was God speaking through my friends. I hated to agree, because I was fatigued and because the thought of rewriting my entire speech twenty-four hours before the drop-dead deadline gave me hives.

But I knew that God had spoken through two of my closest friends and I knew that telling the story of the Golden Fish would have to be done at another time. This time, in front of the president and first lady and vice president and everyone else, I would need to talk about Bonhoeffer and Wilberforce. Got it.

And so, with what little energy and enthusiasm I brought to the task, I started all over again and began hammering out some thoughts and sentences. But it was now Tuesday afternoon, and Wednesday morning we would need to pack and go to the airport. When was I supposed to get this done? I had no idea, but I did what I could, always trusting that the Lord had my back, that he was the one who had something to say and would say it. If I hadn't really known that, rewriting the talk would have been impossible. But I did know it.

So on Tuesday afternoon I e-mailed the folks at the National Prayer Breakfast, letting them know I wouldn't be able to send them the transcript that day, I had to rewrite everything, and I would get them something by five o'clock Wednesday afternoon, on the eve of the breakfast. Surely the translators who wanted to see it would be able to make do with getting it on Wednesday at five, even though it was the last minute. Besides, what could I do?

The next morning as we were getting ready to leave for the airport, I tried to work on it some more. In the midst of packing, I spied a few copies of my Bonhoeffer book and got an idea. Shouldn't I give a signed copy of that book—and perhaps my Wilberforce book as well—to the president and first lady? After all, I'd given copies to George and Laura Bush. Perhaps I should bring along a copy of each of my books, just in case the opportunity presented itself. I doubted it would, but who knew? So I decided to pack them. I wouldn't tell a soul, mainly because I doubted myself whether I would go through with it. But at least I had them with me, and I could decide later.

On the ride to the airport my wife, Susanne, made it clear that whatever I did, I mustn't say a word in my speech about it being her birthday the next day, the day of the breakfast. She was emphatic about this. I knew her real fear was that I would point her out and ask her to stand. That I wouldn't do. But as with the books, I had another crazy idea about how to handle this. I wasn't about to share it with a soul. Only with Nancy Pelosi, as we shall see.

Later that morning when we got on the plane to fly to DC, I still wasn't done with my speech. So I opened my computer on the plane and continued working on it. The plane ride was all of forty minutes, but it's amazing how much you can get done when you are focused and like, totally freaked out, man.

The minute we walked into the lobby of the hotel in DC, I began bumping into people I knew. And not just my aunt and uncle—who had flown up from Atlanta to be with my mom and dad, who were flying down from Danbury, Connecticut—but all kinds of friends, old and new, that I hadn't seen in a long time. The National Prayer Breakfast always creates a buzz of activity in the hotel lobby, and even though most of the people who greeted me didn't know I was to be the speaker the next morning and I couldn't tell them, it was like old home week. But I needed to finish my speech, so eventually I pulled myself away and bade my wife and daughter adieu. They would visit with my mom and dad and aunt and uncle while I kept working on the speech in the hotel room.

As I was working on it, I realized I would need to find a way to print it out. I know that some people thrive on this last-minute sort of thing. I am not one of them. In fact, I despise it and resent it and loathe it with every fiber of my being—and that's putting the best face on it that I can. It tends to make me sick, and I wish I meant that metaphorically. Nonetheless, that's the way this had worked out, and so I tried to practice what I preached, releasing it all to the Lord.

I kept noodling with the speech until—at long last—there was no longer any point to further noodling. After all, one prefers one's speeches *al dente*. Around 3:45 or so I finally said *basta* and sent what I had to the folks who had been waiting for it for more than a week. Did they think it would *ever* arrive? I then printed out a couple of copies via the hotel printers and got dressed and went back down to the lobby, avoiding eye contact with friends, and I then took a cab to the *other* Hilton while my wife and daughter took my parents and aunt and uncle to dinner.

The joy of being at the CCCU event at the other Hilton on Wednesday night was that for a few hours at least I could forget all about the National Prayer Breakfast and my impending speech. It was wonderful to have a respite from thinking about it, to exist in a realm where my focus had to be elsewhere.

But as soon as I arrived at this other Hilton I bumped into my old friend Terry Mattingly, a journalism professor in DC, and, of course, I had to tell *him* about the prayer breakfast and that I was to be the speaker. After all, it was only hours away! And then I bumped into another old friend, Joe Stowell, who used to be president of Moody Bible Institute and who is now the head of Cornerstone University, and, of course, I had to tell *him*! And I bumped into Gaylen Byker of Calvin College and I had to tell *him*; and then I bumped into Union University's David Dockery, and I had to tell *him*. And then I bumped into Michael Lindsay of Gordon College, and I had to tell *him*. And then I bumped into Biola president Barry Corey, who was introducing me, and I had to tell *him*! It was all hopeless.

And, of course, when he introduced me, Barry just *had* to mention it to the crowd! And when it was time for me to speak, now that the cat was out of the bag, there was no reasonable way that I could avoid mentioning it. The idea that I was now speaking to a crowd of Christian college and university presidents, and in just a few hours I would be addressing the president of the United States of America was just too much to hold in. This was the night before the event itself! Surely I could publicly mention what would be news in just a few hours? And so I did. After my speech to them, the crowd of Christian university presidents and their spouses offered to pray for me and did so, actually laying hands on me. To say that I was grateful for this is sheer understatement.

As soon as the CCCU event was over, I said my hurried good-byes and hustled out to get a cab back to the Washington Hilton. There I would assiduously avoid making eye contact with anyone in the lobby, lest I start talking to old friends again and delay getting to sleep, which if you have to get up at 5:00 a.m. and give a speech in front of the president, is somewhat important. I was just at the elevators when I spotted my wife and daughter, who had thrown our family plans under the bus and were still chatting with friends in the lobby. I urgently pressed them to come with me to the elevator so we could all go to sleep. They probably didn't realize it, but I was to be the keynote speaker at the prayer breakfast in the morning and I had hoped to be as fresh as possible for the task ahead! Susanne said she would follow in five minutes, so I took Annerose and got on the elevator.

A lovely couple got on with us and engaged my daughter in conversation. Not only did the woman speak Greek, but her husband, who was also in the elevator with us, was Greek royalty. As we got off the elevator with them, they explained that they lived—presumably in exile—in a palace in Belgrade. When my daughter realized we were talking to an actual princess, she went googly-eyed. I had tried to tell her there would be dignitaries from around the world, but now, on the very eve of the breakfast, she had firsthand evidence. The woman gave us her card, which detailed their royal credentials, and we exchanged a few more pleasantries in Greek.

Before we parted, I blurted to the woman and her husband that in a few hours I would be the speaker at the breakfast. Who could contain such a thing, I ask you? But lo! near the tenth-floor elevator that very moment there lurked behind an arras, like Polonius, someone who had overheard me. (Actually there was no arras, nor had I any poniard.) But as it happened, he was one of the people who is part of the group that puts on the breakfast, and who had, in fact, instructed me not to breathe a word about the fact that I was the speaker *until the morning of the breakfast.* Man, was I busted or what? But what could I do? So off to bed I went and fell asleep reasonably early. So far, so good.

Unfortunately just a few hours later I woke up. The clock said that it was 3:00 a.m. And somehow I knew I wasn't about to go back to sleep anytime soon. I don't think it was nervous energy. I simply think the room was too warm. But knowing that the alarm was set to go off at 5:00 made it unlikely that I would fall back to sleep. So for the next two hours I lay there, praying and wondering why the Lord would allow me to only get a few hours sleep in advance of my important talk. Nonetheless, he did.

As I cast about for a biblical cognate, I think of when the Lord thinned Gideon's army down to three hundred men. To the human mind it seems insane, but God always has a plan. In the case of Gideon, he wanted to make a point about who is in charge of the battle. I lay there, trying to trust God with what lay ahead, and at 5:00 a.m. the alarm went off, and that was that. I leapt out of bed. I knew that I would be dead tired and genuinely—literally—dizzy for lack of sleep. But the show must go on.

At 6:35 there was an officious knock at the door. It was the aides who were to escort us to the ballroom. They had told me they would come to fetch us at 6:45, but evidently National Prayer Breakfast aides like to err on the early side of punctuality. I told them we would be ready in just a few minutes and then shut the door. My parents and aunt and uncle arrived, bright-eyed and bushy-tailed as only senior citizens can be at that hour. At last we were all ready. I grabbed the two books I had secretly signed the day before. Would the aides let me take them to the stage? Everyone who was going to the prayer breakfast had been strictly informed that they couldn't take anything into the ballroom. Nothing—not a camera, not a cell phone, not a purse. It seemed kind of crazy, but they were quite serious about it. When you are in close proximity to the president of the United States, the standard rules of life change. But I needed those books! If they gave me a hard time, I would insist I needed them, that they were props in my comedy routine, which they were, in a way.

The aides escorted us to a secret elevator—it was the service elevator—and the young man in charge of this security detail spoke soberly into his sleeve. "We have the keynote speaker on the elevator," he said. I'd never been the object of words spoken into a sleeve before, and I marked this moment in my mind as some kind of milestone. We got off that elevator and walked to another service elevator. It was all somehow baroque. I had a funny feeling that at any minute we would find ourselves in an underground bunker with Dick Cheney. Eventually we emerged and were escorted down other secret corridors and then through a large kitchen. I now expected to be taken to a front-row table at the Copacabana, with Jerry Vale singing "*Non Dimenticar*." Henny Youngman would be in the wings with his violin.

Finally we emerged into what seemed like the hotel again, and I saw the crowds making their way into the vast ballroom nearby. It was now time for me to peel away from my family. Susanne could have come with me, but she had weeks earlier elected not to sit on the dais, where C-Span cameras would have been trained on her. Instead she would sit anonymously in the crowd with our family. They were all escorted away from me, toward the ballroom, and I was led in another direction. I realized I was being taken to some super-secured secret area behind the stage, where the president and vice president and others would be gathering. I could see by the grim, pinched looks on people's faces as we passed that we were now approaching that fabled zone. Then, suddenly, there we were. Where were we, exactly? We were just about to go into a specially cordoned-off area just behind the stage.

But before I entered that area, I wanted to peek out through the curtains to see the ballroom itself. Somewhere out there were my parents and my wife and daughter, and my aunt and uncle, and so many friends. I was now allowed to walk out onto the stage, accompanied by the aides who had brought me here. But because of the bright lights shining toward the stage, I couldn't see much. As I stood on the stage, one of the presidential aides put the president's speech, which was in a binder, on the podium. I told him that I would have to put my notes on the podium when I spoke, and my notes obviously couldn't lie flat on the tilted vinyl surface of the presidential binder. I could see this presented a difficulty. I marveled at the pressure these presidential aides must be under. In any case, the binder containing the president's speech was removed.

I was taken backstage again and entered that special cordoned-off section. The first thing I noticed was that there were chairs along the wall, each with the name of one of the people who were to be seated on the dais. One simply said "The President" and another "The First Lady." Another said "The Vice President." Another "Senator Sessions." Another "Mrs. Sessions." Another said "Nancy Pelosi." One of them had my name on it. And then the names of all the others who would be on the dais. Someone explained that they were arranged just as we were seated on the dais, because when it was time to go out we would need to line up in that order and proceed to our seats.

Eventually Senator Sessions arrived and greeted me warmly, as did Senator Mark Pryor. Their wives were with them. And now Nancy Pelosi arrived. It was an odd thing seeing her there, because in my mind she is "Nancy Pelosi," someone from TV with whom I diverge on political issues, but here she was in the flesh, just another person, chatting with the others about to go out onto the stage. I said hello, and we struck up a conversation. Because of my lack of sleep, I was in a very jokey mood. I'm not sure, but she was probably wondering who the odd fellow in the suit was. I almost quipped that

I'd gotten my suit from a Chicago gangster. And no, it wasn't Rahm Emmanuel. Ha-ha. But I thought better of it. I did, however, ask to take a picture with her.

There were now still a few minutes before we would have to go out. Again, I peeked out onto the stage. A presidential aide told me that I couldn't go out there now. It had been "secured," or something along those lines, and was now officially off limits. So I returned to the gaggle of those waiting behind the stage and saw that Vice President Joe Biden had arrived. But where was the president? Evidently he was still on his way. Would he blame his tardiness on George W. Bush? Ha-ha. *Easy there, fella.* I couldn't stop kidding! This could get me into trouble.

At last it was time to go out. We lined up like an elementary school class, in the order of our names on the wall. I realized I was next to Vice President Biden, another person with whom I diverged politically and who had often been the subject of my jokes. But here he was, in the flesh. At last we marched out and took our seats. The ballroom was now filled with thousands of people. By shielding my eyes from the light and squinting, I was able to make out some people I knew. My wife and daughter and parents were far to my left. Right in front of me was the Greek woman we had met in the elevator the night before. She seemed to have the best seat in the house! And just behind her was none other than Secretary of State Hillary Clinton, who had spoken at the National Prayer Breakfast a few years earlier, as had former Secretary of State Condoleezza Rice and Senator Joseph Lieberman and so many others in political life.

On the dais I found myself seated next to the vice president. He was on my right. On his right was Senator Pryor, who was next to the podium. To my left was Senator Pryor's wife, chatting with Nancy Pelosi, to her left.

I realized that I ought to be talking to the vice president. But what should I say? Because of my pronounced lack of sleep, this was more difficult than it normally would have been. I was reeling with dizziness and fatigue, and all I could think of was a brilliantly hilarious piece I had read in the *Onion* magazine, featuring a photoshopped shirtless Joe Biden washing his Trans-Am in the White House driveway. It was so dead-on perfect and funny that it had even inspired me to write a piece just like it. At one point, for lack of anything else to say, I bravely asked the vice president if he had seen those humorous bits about himself in the *Onion*. I knew he had a good sense of humor, so I wasn't afraid to bring it up. And he said that yes, he had seen them, and he didn't mind them at all, because they were so obviously about someone who was completely different from what he was really like.

Even in my sleep-deprived stupor, I was quite sure he was mistaken in this, but one doesn't argue with a vice president. Certainly not at that hour. Then he added, as a kind of Q.E.D: "For one thing, I hate Camaros!" When you haven't had enough sleep, your mind can play tricks. Had the vice president of the United States really just told me emphatically that he hated Camaros? Yes, he had. I was sure of it. But the cognitive dissonance was almost painful, because this was precisely the sort of thing I would have made up about him in a humor piece. Except it was true, he had really said that. Truth is always stranger than fiction.

A few more minutes passed. But where were the president and first lady? They still weren't there. And so the chit-chatting continued. I suddenly realized I hadn't let Nancy Pelosi in on my little joke about pretending to the crowd that she was my wife. My plan was to announce that it was my wife's birthday and then gesture to the former Speaker and she would rise a bit and wave and that would be that. Of course most folks would realize it was a joke. As my fatigued mind took over, I told her about my idea.

"When I get up," I said, "I'm going to pretend you're my wife, just as a little joke, so if you don't mind, just wave or something." By now she could see very well that I was plum loco, so she just smiled vaguely and shook her head, as if to say, *oh, you wouldn't really do that!* But of course I would! Didn't she know how little sleep I had had and what a cut-up I was in general? It would be hilarious! Pretending Nancy Pelosi was my wife! In front of thousands of people. *It would kill!* Trust me, Nancy, this is comedy gold! But I didn't say anything like that. I didn't want to push it. I was sure when the time came the former Speaker of the House would sense the tremendous comedic potential and would dutifully rise or give a little wave, to pretend that she was my wife. This would let me mention it was my wife's birthday without actually embarrassing my wife! It was brilliant!

In any case, soon the president and first lady arrived. You may already know this, but when the president of the United States arrives anywhere in the United States, everyone stands, as we now did. Everyone in the whole room stood, and seven thousand eyes were fixed on the most powerful man in the world as he waved and finally took his seat for breakfast. I had been so far away the last two times the two previous presidents had entered this room at the breakfasts, but this time I was just a few feet away. It was hard not to be amazed at my proximity to him. I had never been near a sitting president before. Pun *almost* intended.

I must say here that I had been given the honor and privilege of spending a full hour with George W. Bush a year before. It was at his new post-presidential office in a Dallas high-rise. It was a tremendous blessing to get to do that. The meeting came about because he and the first lady had read my Bonhoeffer book sometime in 2010. The first lady had spoken about this publicly a few times. And in the fall of 2010 I had received a handwritten note from the president, thanking me for the signed copy I had sent to him and the first lady. A while after getting this letter—which I've since framed—I e-mailed the aide who worked in his office. I said that I traveled to Dallas frequently and I wondered whether I might ever be able to meet the president. I would be in Dallas the following week and a few more times in the coming months. I assumed this was all a bit of a long shot. But in short order I was connected with the woman who kept his schedule and she told me that I was to show up at their office at 9:00 a.m. the following Monday. This was staggering news.

That Monday in Dallas I drove my rental car to the address given me and got to meet President George W. Bush, who was as jaunty and personable and relaxed as I imagined he might be. He was an early riser, and I believe he had just come from playing golf or mountain biking. We talked for an hour about Bonhoeffer and other things. He is, in fact, an avid reader, and our talk ranged over a variety of subjects. Toward the end of our time we were joined by an aide who had also read my book and who wanted to join the conversation. When it was time to leave, we had a photo taken, and it was my goofy idea to have the president hold my Bonhoeffer book, while

I held his book, which I was reading at the time and which he signed for me. Just before I left I asked if I might pray for him, which I did, laying a hand on his shoulder. It was a moving thing and a profound honor to do so.

Now, almost exactly a year later, I was a few feet away from another president. And in a few moments I would rise to speak in front of him. I looked at the program. There were still a few more things that must happen before it was time for the keynote speech. Nancy Pelosi rose to read Scripture. Senator Daniel Akaka of Hawaii spoke. Eleven-year-old Jackie Evancho sang a song. But finally, eventually, it was my turn. Senator Mark Pryor introduced me, and I rose.

And now, ladies and gentlemen, the proverbial money shot . . .
I still can't believe this really happened. Nor can my publisher
(Thomas Nelson) who foolishly agreed to a clause in my contract
that said if I could get a sitting US president to publicly display
my book (cover outward) in a public setting with 3,000 or more
persons in attendance and a US senator within six feet, they
would pay me a **one-million-dollar** bonus. Of course
every penny of it will go to charity, because that's just how I roll.

With appreciation to Rick Potter of Potter Photo Studios for permission to use

2

THE NATIONAL PRAYER BREAKFAST ADDRESS

What follows is an annotated transcript of the National Prayer Breakfast address, delivered February 2, 2012.

Well, good morning to all of you: honored guests from around the world and from this great nation. And especially to our president and first lady. What an honor to be here!

Now I would love to know how many people are here this morning. If you don't mind, just indulge me. If you are here this morning, would you raise your hand? I just want to get a quick count. Okay, I think I counted four. Well, they claimed there would be about four *thousand. . . .* [*]

So let me just say up front that I am not a morning person.

But it is nonetheless an honor to speak at this august—and extraordinarily early—gathering. I know it is an august gathering because they charged $175 for breakfast! [**]

I don't want to start out by being negative, but I think there may be some kind of money laundering thing happening here. I am speaking truth to power, people! The price gouging—it needs to stop! Even as a member of the elite 1 percent, I cannot afford this. [***]

But you know, we joke. Yes, we joke. But seriously, I know who puts these events on. They are a highly secret—indeed a downright nefarious—organization. They call themselves "the Family." Yes,

---

[*] I do a lot of public speaking and I've tried out this goofy joke many times. Usually about a third of the people present raise their hands. But this time, perhaps because it was so early and because most of the people were not expecting goofy humor from the keynote speaker at the National Prayer Breakfast, just a tiny handful of people raised their hands. Nonetheless, I soldiered on.

[**] This is the real price of the breakfast, although at any event featuring the president of the United States and first lady and countless other luminaries, this is probably about the going rate.

[***] Just outside the Hilton Hotel, where the National Prayer Breakfast is held, there were many self-styled Occupy Wall Street protestors, protesting against the breakfast. As with the larger OWS movement, they were claiming to speak for the 99 percent of Americans and against the 1 percent they scorned as wealthy elitists.

"the Family." You see "the Family" not only runs this event, they run everything that is happening in the world.*

We—and of course I mean, the president and I, specifically—are all their puppets. The president knows what I mean; he cannot admit this publicly, obviously. But appearing here this morning, we are simply doing their bidding.

Every US president has been elected by them—except for Warren G. Harding. No one knows how Harding was able to buck that trend, but we know that he paid dearly for it—most notably by being saddled with the name Warren G. Harding.

A brief word on the dais thing up here. I am not a politician, so when I see a dais like this I immediately think of those wonderful Dean Martin Roasts from the 1970s.**

Those were my favorite shows—right next to *Sanford and Son*. I am being honest with you now. So you'll forgive me if I pretend that I am up here with Ruth Buzzi, Bob Hope, Jimmy Stewart, Red Buttons, Charlie Callas, Foster Brooks, and Rich Little.***

---

* In a cover story in *Harper's* magazine and in a subsequent book titled *The Family*, the writer Jeff Sharlet seriously claimed to have exposed the group who put on these National Prayer Breakfasts as a powerful theocratic cabal, bent on world domination. Needless to say, having gotten to know many of the men and women who are a part of the Fellowship, I was hard-pressed to buy this thesis and thought I could use the occasion to make light of it. As with many of my more inside jokes, only a minority in the audience knew what I was actually lampooning.

** About once a month in the 1970s, the singer and actor Dean Martin would host a comic roast of some celebrity, which would air on network TV. These events were mostly held at Caesar's Palace in Las Vegas and boasted a Who's Who of luminaries from the Golden Age of Hollywood (Jack Benny, George Burns, and Lucille Ball) along with TV stars popular that year (Redd Foxx, Angie Dickinson, Freddie Prinz, and Gabe Kaplan). The participants were always seated on a long dais, and each would rise in turn and go to the podium to make fun of the "Man of the Hour," who could be anyone from Ronald Reagan to Howard Cosell to Sammy Davis Junior.

*** I'm sure anyone in the audience who was not in the United States in the seventies—and this would include a great percentage of the audience, which included ambassadors and heads of state from around the world—had no idea what I was talking about. One can only imagine what the ambassador from Yemen would make of my mentioning Ruth Buzzi!

I am being honest: that is who I *wish* were up here.

And to those who are actually up here, I apologize. From the bottom of Don Rickles' heart, I'm sorry.[*]

Now, this *is* National Prayer Breakfast, so maybe we should get serious and say something about prayer. . . . *Nah.*

Okay, but seriously. *What is prayer*? That's the real question that we must ask ourselves: *What is prayer*?

Prayer is real faith in God. It is not phony religiosity. It is not: "O! wouldst thou, O Sovereign of the universe, take this archaic verbiage as evidence that we believe that thou art an old fashioned and unpleasant and easily annoyed—and even cranky—deity! And that to get thy magnificent attention and so as to not *annoy* thee, we must needs employ an archaic and religious sounding language."

That, my friends, is not prayer. That is—to use the current terminology—a lot of "pious baloney."[**]

Who said that? I believe it was Nancy Pelosi? It was someone on the couch. I can't remember.[***]

But the point is that that sort of "pious baloney" is not prayer. It is not faith in the God of Scripture. Just imagine talking to Jesus that

---

[*] Don Rickles is a comedian who appeared on most of the Dean Martin roasts and who has always been known for insulting those around him and for then dishonestly saying that he was sorry for doing so. I felt deeply honored to be able to follow in his footsteps, if only for a few derisive paces.

[**] In one of the GOP primary debates that had just taken place prior to the 2012 National Prayer Breakfast, former Speaker of the House Newt Gingrich had famously derided something that Governor Mitt Romney had said as "pious baloney."

[***] Another mostly inside joke. During the GOP primary, many of Newt Gingrich's detractors had tried to remind voters of an infamous television commercial that he had made some years before in which he had sat on a couch with Congresswoman Nancy Pelosi. It was an attempt to show that he could be bi-partisan, but his opponents were using it as a cudgel, to show that he was not a true conservative. Adding to the dumb joke was the fact that Nancy Pelosi was sitting a few feet away from me as I delivered these remarks, and I knew that she and everyone in the Washington, DC, political class would be in on the joke. I hoped that at least they would find it funny.

way! He would almost laugh at you. Imagine if we talked to him that way.

Prayer is from the heart. We can't try to fool God with phony religiosity. Adam and Eve tried that with a fig leaf once. It did not go so well.[*]

And this gets to my theme this morning: the difference between mere religion—or religiosity—and real faith in God.

We all know people who go to church who do not show the love of Jesus. We know people who know Scripture, but who sometimes use it as a weapon. Real prayer, real faith is not religious. It is from the heart. It is honest. It is real. I have had the privilege of writing about two men—Wilberforce and Bonhoeffer—whose lives illustrate the difference between mere religiosity and actually knowing and serving God.

Let me first quickly tell you personally how I came to see the difference between these two utterly different things.

———

First of all, I am the son of European immigrants who met in an English class in New York City in 1956. And I thank the Lord that my parents are in the room this morning. *Please don't get up.*

———

[*] Adam and Eve's efforts to conceal their nakedness with aprons of fig leaves is the original and classic illustration of the difference between "dead religion" and a "saving faith" in the God of Scripture. It is the first picture we have of how human beings' efforts are insufficient and cannot fool God. Before Adam and Eve were banished from Eden, God provided animal skins for them, replacing the aprons of fig leaves. This substitution by God himself, which involves the taking of innocent life, prefigures the substitution of Jesus for us. It illustrates that in order for us to be "covered" appropriately, innocent blood must be shed. Our own efforts—fig leaves—cannot do it. In Eden and in the Old Testament it is the blood of animals that "covers" our sins, and in the New Testament and thereafter, it is the blood of Jesus.

My dad is Greek, hence my surname Metaxas. My mom is German, hence my deep love for Siegfried and Roy.* Thank you.

Now, when you have one Greek parent, you are raised Greek. Forget about the German part! Greeks believe that being Greek is the most important thing in the world. Now I am obviously 50 percent Greek. I have always tried to be *more* than 50 percent Greek, but somehow I have never been able to break the 50 percent barrier. A little bit like brother Mitt. . . .** [*Looking over at the president.*] I thought you might like that one. Good.

So I grew up, of course, in the Greek Orthodox Church. I was an altar boy. And I had a modicum of faith. But it was mostly a nominal, cultural faith. I thought of myself as a Christian of some sort.

And then I went to Yale University.***

Of course, that is the dream come true of every son of working class European immigrants. But the reality is that Yale—and most of our universities, but especially Yale—is a very secular place. Aggressively secular. And what little modicum of faith I had was seriously challenged.

At Yale, the idea of God was essentially ignored—or sneered at.

---

* Another ridiculous dumb joke, doubtless lost on the hundreds of foreign attendees that morning. Siegfried and Roy were a pair of flamboyantly attired tiger and lion tamers whose act in Las Vegas— along with multiple television appearances—made them household words, until their act was tragically ended by a tiger attack in October 2003.

** Another political joke. Former Massachusetts governor Mitt Romney had been consistently leading the GOP primary polls, and was thought to be President Obama's likely opponent in the fall, but he was frustrated in never being able to get a commanding 50 percent or more majority, which would have established him as the frontrunner and would have finally sidelined his many opponents. It was also believed that having to continue slugging it out with his opponents would weaken him in the general election in the fall.

*** I graduated Yale in 1984, with a degree in English Literature. While there I was the editor of the *Yale Record*, the nation's oldest college humor magazine.

By the time I had graduated, I was quite sure that it was wrong to be serious about the Bible, or to take Jesus seriously, and that it was all hopelessly parochial and divisive. I wasn't sure what was supposed to replace it. I guess I was confused. I was lost.

I knew that I wanted to be a writer. But I was not terribly successful. I floundered. Then I drifted. Then I floundered some more. Then I drifted and floundered simultaneously. Don't think that was easy!

Eventually things got so bad that I moved back in with my parents. Which I do not recommend. I *specifically* don't recommend moving in with *my* parents.

I joke, but it was in fact a very tough time for me. I am being serious now. I suffered during that period from real, genuine depression. I still struggle with that. Those were genuinely painful, soul-searching times in my life. Very painful. I took a really depressing job, which my parents *forced* me to take.[*]

And while I was at this job—this miserable job—by the way, thank you Mom and Dad! Thank you—while I was at this miserable job, I met a man of some faith and he began to share his faith with me, with the twenty-four-year-old secular Yale agnostic. And I was in enough pain that I was willing to listen a little bit to what he had to say. He was an Episcopalian, so I figured it was safe. After all, they don't really believe that stuff anyway. *Please.*

---

[*] I was teasing my parents, who were in the room. The job I took during this painful period was that of a proofreader in the corporate headquarters of Union Carbide, the international chemical conglomerate, located in Danbury, Connecticut, where I grew up. I worked there for precisely one year, reading endless copy of the most boring sort imaginable in a fluorescent-lit cubicle I have always described as "a quarter-mile from the nearest window." The exaggeration is only slight.

So I effectively said to him: keep talking. But he turned out to be one of those Episcopalians who actually believed the stuff! And he knew the Bible backward and forward, and I was really challenged. We would have a lot of conversations. I was not exactly ready to accept what he was saying. I was not ready to pray, go to Bible study, go to church, or to become a weird born-again Christian. Like many of *you*. I was not ready, but I was in enough pain to keep listening.*

And this friend of mine said to me that I should pray that God would reveal himself to me. Which seemed absurd, because I thought, *I don't know if he is there, so I don't really want to pray to the oxygen in the room. To whom shall I pray if he is not there*? It is a conundrum, as you can see. But sometimes you are in enough pain—and I was—to do unreasonable things. And so once in a while, I would pray, and I said in my anguish—and it was very real anguish—I said, *God if you are there, please reveal yourself to me! Punch a hole through the sheet rock! Wave to me. Say hello. Show yourself to me!*

I was desperate. Every now and again I would pray that prayer. I would be jogging and I would pray that prayer: *God, help me. I need help.*

It was an honest prayer. And prayers come from a place of honesty, not religiosity. If you can say *Help me, Lord*, God hears that prayer.

And then, around my twenty-fifth birthday, I had a dream. We don't have time to go into it this morning, but it was an amazing dream. I am not making this up. If you want to hear the story of this amazing dream, you can go to my website, which is just my name, if

---

* The man who befriended me was the then-thirty-one-year-old Ed Tuttle, an extremely talented graphic designer and fine artist. We remain close friends to this day.

you can spell it. It is www.EricMetaxas.com. If you can't spell it, it's *still* www.EricMetaxas.com.

But it was an amazing dream, and it changed my life. God came into my life. Jesus came into my life. And it's all true, except for the part about the UFO and the Sasquatch—which I just made up. But seriously, watch that short video, if you don't mind, because it really happened. It is not made up.*

And when God came into my life, literally overnight, and answered that prayer, I wondered, *Why hadn't I heard this before? Why did I have to suffer not knowing? Why? Why?*

And I think part of the reason is that I had rejected a phony, religious idea of God. Not God as he really is. Because when I encountered God as he really is, I knew that that was what my heart was longing for. That was the answer! He was the answer to my pain and all my questions. He was real. And he loved me, despite everything I have done.

I saw that he is not some moral code. He is not some energy force. He is alive, he is a person. He knows everything about me. And about you. He knows my story. He knows your story. Every detail. He knows your deepest fears.

He knows the terrible selfish things you have done that have hurt others. And he still loves you! And he knows the hurt that others have caused *you*. He knows us. He is alive. He is not a joy-killing bummer, or some moralistic "church lady." He is the most wonderful Person— capital *P*—imaginable! In fact, his name is *Wonderful . . .***

---

* This video is part of the spectacular "New Birth Portraits" series, commissioned by Redeemer Presbyterian Church in Manhattan, where Tim Keller is the senior pastor.
** The reference is to Isaiah 9:6: "And his name shall be called Wonderful, Counsellor, Almighty God, the Everlasting Father, the Prince of Peace" (KJV). Many people know this scripture from Handel's *Messiah*.

Now, who would reject that?

So at that point I realized that everything I had rejected about God was actually not God. It was just dead religion. It was phoniness; it was people who go to church and do not show the love of Jesus. It was people who know the Bible and use it as a weapon. People who don't practice what they preach. People who are indifferent to the poor and suffering. People who use religion as a way to exclude others from their group. People who use religion as a way to judge others.

I had rejected that. But guess what? Jesus had *also* rejected that. He had railed against that. And he called people to real life and real faith. Jesus was and is the enemy of dead religion.

That is true. That is not a point of view.

He came to deliver us from that. He railed against the religious leaders of his day because he knew it was all just a front. That in their hearts they were far from God, his Father.

When he was tempted in the desert, who was the one throwing Bible verses at him? Satan. That is a perfect picture of dead religion. Using the words of God to do the opposite of what God does. It is grotesque, when you think about it. It is demonic.

That summer, as I came to faith, the guy who shared his faith with me, Ed Tuttle, gave me a copy of *The Cost of Discipleship* by Dietrich Bonhoeffer. And he asked me if I had ever heard of Bonhoeffer, and I said no. And he said, "Well, Bonhoeffer was a pastor, who because of his faith in Jesus, stood up for the Jews of Europe." I was absolutely shocked.

My mother is German. She grew up during this period.[*]

Why had I never heard this amazing story about Bonhoeffer before? I remember thinking somebody really ought to write a book about him! But I was not interested in writing biographies. I am far too self-centered to spend that much time focusing on someone besides myself.

So I went on to have a strange career. I wrote children's books. I wrote humor for the *New York Times*. I worked for VeggieTales. Yes, VeggieTales! *Thank you*. Oh yes, *now* you are listening.[**]

And then I wanted to share my faith, and I wrote a book with a ridiculous title: *Everything You Always Wanted to Know About God But Were Afraid to Ask*. Actually it's a trilogy—three books.[***]

And then one day I found myself being interviewed about this book on CNN.[****]

I was expecting a really tough question, like "How can a good God allow evil and suffering?" But instead I got a softball question,

---

[*] My mother was raised in Altenburg, near Leipzig. In 1944, when she was nine, her father, Erich Kraegen, was killed in the war, while traveling to the Russian front. He was a genuinely reluctant German soldier, who before he was called up would secretly listen to the BBC with his ear literally pressed against the radio speaker. If a German was caught listening to foreign radio broadcasts during this time, he could be sent to a concentration camp. The pain that Hitler and the war caused my family has been a part of the background of my life, and my desire to write a book about Bonhoeffer comes, in part, from this desire to understand what happened during this tragic period in recent history.

[**] VeggieTales videos are so popular that whenever I publicly mention that I worked there as a writer, the audience reaction is dramatic. Often there are whoops and cheers, as there was in this instance. I wrote the Omlet/Hamlet half of the *Lyle the Kindly Viking* video, and wrote several VeggieTales books, including *God Made You Special*. I am also privileged to have been selected as the voice of the narrator on the Esther video. The folks at VeggieTales liked my reading so much that still to this day, twelve years later, I remain the voice of the narrator on that video. *Ahem*.

[***] The first book (Waterbrook, 2005) is titled *Everything You Always Wanted to Know About God (But Were Afraid to Ask)*. The second book (Waterbrook, 2007) is titled *Everything ELSE You Always Wanted to Know About God (But Were Afraid to Ask)*. And the third book (Regal, 2010) is titled *Everything You Always Wanted to Know About God (But Were Afraid to Ask): The Jesus Edition*.

[****] This was in December 2005, and the CNN anchor who interviewed me was Keira Phillips. The video of this segment is available on my website: www.EricMetaxas.com.

for which I was quite unprepared. The CNN host said to me, "You know there is something in here about Wilberforce." I had maybe two sentences in the whole book about Wilberforce. And she asked me, "Can you talk about that?" Suddenly I was on CNN being asked to talk about Wilberforce! All I knew about Wilberforce was in the book, was that he was someone who took the Bible so seriously that he changed the world forever. So I start talking about him briefly and the next thing I know a publisher calls me up and says there is a movie coming out called *Amazing Grace*. I'm sure you know the *song* "Amazing Grace." Yes, we will sing it later.*

I didn't write that song. I just want to be clear. It was, of course, written by the fabulous Mr. Tony Bennett! Is he here?**

But seriously, I was asked to write a book about Wilberforce. And amazingly, I wrote a biography about him, and everywhere I went talking about Wilberforce people would say to me, "Who are you going to write about next? Who are you going to write about next?"

Some people asked me, "About *whom* will you next write?"

Now, as a Yale English major, I want to recommend the word *whom*. If English is your first language—and for some of you in here it is indeed your first language—you may want to use the word *whom*. You can get it free as an app on your iPhone. You just download it. You can use it as much as you want.

But seriously, I would get that question constantly: *Eric, about whom will you next write?*

And I thought, well, there is only one person besides Wilberforce

---

* Of course, the audience thought I was joking, and laughed, but indeed I was *not* joking.
** Tony Bennett had not written this famous song. It was written by John Newton, a former slave ship captain turned pastor. Of course, this was a joke.

William Wilberforce

about whom I would write *if* I were to write a second biography. I was thinking about Bonhoeffer. And, of course, I did write that book, and I have to tell you nobody is more shocked by the reception of the book than I. No one is more grateful to the Lord for the people who are reading and talking about this book.

I know that it was read even by President George W. Bush,* who is intellectually incurious, as we have all read.**

He read the book. [*Glancing toward President Obama.*] No pressure. I just want to say *no pressure.* [*Here I handed a copy of* Bonhoeffer *to Senator Jeff Sessions, who passed it to the president, seated next to him. The president held it up and smiled. Applause.*]***

I know you are very busy, Mr. President, but I know sometimes you take plane rides and you have time to kill. So here. [*I then handed him a copy of* Amazing Grace: William Wilberforce and the Heroic Campaign to End Slavery.] No pressure. No pressure at all. Who am I to pressure *you*?****

---

* In the fall of 2010 I was speaking at an event in Dallas, when a man privately told me that some weeks before at his Dallas country club, George and Laura Bush had stopped by. The gentleman claimed he had personally overheard the former president talking about my Bonhoeffer book—and said that he had even praised the writing. Needless to say I was flabbergasted and flattered and I suppose a tiny bit incredulous too. But it was all true. As I mentioned earlier, just a few weeks later I received in the mail a handwritten note from the former president, extolling the book. As a result of this I was privileged to meet with the former president in his Dallas office some weeks later. I spent nearly an hour with him, discussing Bonhoeffer and many other subjects, including the prospects for the 2012 elections. When we parted he even generously offered to provide a video greeting for the Canterbury Medal Awards Dinner at which I was honored in May 2011.
** Of course, I was joking. The media had often portrayed him this way, and that infamous phrase "intellectually incurious" was first put forth in a book, written by David Frum, a former speechwriter for Dick Cheney. But my experience with the former president—and the testimony of many who know him well—is that he is anything but that. By all accounts, he is a voracious reader, which is not so surprising when one considers that he married a librarian. That librarian—Laura Bush—has also read the book, as had others in the former president's close circle. When a friend of mine met the president at an event in Lakeland, Florida, she mentioned the Bonhoeffer book to him, and he cheerfully told her: "Condi's reading it right now!"
*** I'm glad I was correct in thinking that security might let me take the books in with me since I was the keynote speaker. Although I really had no idea if I would have the courage to actually hand the books to the president as I did. It was a last-minute decision.
**** Anyone who knows me knows that I show affection by kidding around and teasing and that I particularly

Nonetheless, the lives of both of these two men illustrate the difference between phony religiosity and really believing in God in a way that is real, that changes your life. It must change your life and the lives of others.

Now, of course, Wilberforce is best known for leading the movement to end the slave trade. But why did he take that on? Do you know why? I am here to tell you, it was not because he was just a churchgoer. Because there were plenty of churchgoers in England in the day of Wilberforce, and most of them seemed to have no problem with the slave trade or slavery. I'm talking about people who went to *church*.

No, the reason Wilberforce fought so hard against the slave trade was because around his twenty-sixth birthday, he encountered Jesus. Really.

Most people in England paid lip service to God in those days. Everybody said, "I am Christian. I am English. Yes, we are Christians." But somehow most of them really seemed to think that the slave trade was a fine thing.

So keep in mind that when someone says, I am a Christian, it might mean *absolutely nothing.*

But for Wilberforce, it became real. It was not about Christianity. It was about the living God and serving him. And Wilberforce suddenly took the Bible seriously, and the idea that all of us are created in the image of God. He took the idea seriously that it was our duty to care "for the least of these" and he said, "Lord, I will obey."

Now he fought politically. He fought hard. And did you know that the only people really fighting with him at this point were the

love to kid and tease those who are often thought of as too important to kid and tease. So this opportunity to kid around with a sitting president of the United States was especially enjoyable for me.

fanatical Christians? Did you know that? All the churchgoers, all the religious people, they were not alongside him. Who was alongside him in those days? The born-again nuts. The Quakers. The Methodists that people made fun of. *They* were in the trenches, because they knew they had no choice but to regard the Africans as made in the image of God and worthy of our love and respect. Everyone else was just going with the flow. All the people who just went to church, as I say, they got it wrong. They had not seen Jesus.

Wilberforce took these ideas—these foreign ideas from the Bible—and brought them into culture. And you can read about it, not just in my book, which the president may read—but you can read about it elsewhere. These are historical facts. This is not my spin. This is true. Because he believed what the Bible said and because he obeyed what God told him to do, Wilberforce changed the world.

Think of this my friends: today we argue about how to help the poor. Some say, "Oh, the public sector or the government is the answer!" Others say "the private sector, free enterprise!" But today we argue about *how* to help the poor, not *whether* to help the poor! Praise the Lord.

The idea to care for the poor. The idea that slavery is wrong. These ideas are not normal human ideas. These are *biblical* ideas, imported by Wilberforce at a crucial time. Human beings do not do the right thing apart from God's intervention. We always do the phony, religious thing. We go with the flow. In Wilberforce's day, going with the flow meant supporting slavery. That Africans are not fully human. In Bonhoeffer's world, in Nazi Germany, it meant supporting the idea that Jews are not fully human. So who do we say is not fully human today?* Who is expendable to us? Please discuss amongst yourselves.

But back to Nazi Germany. It all happened a moment ago. My mother lived through it. There are other people in this room who lived through it. It was a moment ago. I was in Germany just last week,** and I met a number of people who lived through this period, who were in fact the sons of people I mention in my Bonhoeffer book, who fought against Hitler.*** It was a moment ago that this horror happened.

Now, if you don't know who Bonhoeffer is, let me say very briefly that Bonhoeffer was born in 1906. Actually he was born on February 4, which is two days from now. And it is two days after my wife's birthday. Now she begged me not to mention that her birthday was today, but honey, would you please stand up?****

---

* Ironically and embarrassingly, for all my prating about the word whom, in giving the speech that morning I actually misspoke and said "whom do we say" when I obviously should have said "who do we say"! I believe I was about to say, "So whom do we regard as not fully human today?" That would have been correct. But after I said the word whom I changed course midsentence—I often do that—and the word whom became suddenly and retroactively incorrect.

** The Bonhoeffer book had been published in German a few months earlier, so one week prior to the National Prayer Breakfast, I had been traveling in Switzerland and Germany, talking about Bonhoeffer in a number of venues.

*** While speaking at an event in Wiesbaden the week before the prayer breakfast, two gentlemen had come up to me to introduce themselves. One was the son of Fabian von Schlabrendorf, a man who planted a bomb on Hitler's plane. It had been disguised as a package of brandy. When he learned that the bomb had never exploded, he had to retrieve it, so that it wouldn't be discovered. To meet the son of this hero was a profound honor, as was meeting the second gentleman who approached me that evening. He was the son of Bonhoeffer's famous uncle, General Paul von Hase, who also participated in the conspiracy against Hitler and who was executed following the famous Valkyrie plot in July 1944.

**** Very few people actually know what happened here, and I am more than grateful for the opportunity to tell the real story, which is this: As I said earlier, it was indeed my wife's birthday that day, and I had intended to publicly note this, but Susanne very clearly and in no uncertain terms asked me not to do so. She thought it would be embarrassing, not to mention that it would cut into the short time that I had to give my speech. And, of course, I was prepared to honor her request. But then I had a funny idea. At least I thought it was funny. In fact, I thought it was hilarious. My plan was simply to pretend that Nancy Pelosi was my wife. My wife was seated in the ballroom with my parents and daughter, so when I gestured to the woman sitting on the dais—to Nancy Pelosi—everyone in the room would know that

Sweetie, don't be shy. Come on. Please? She is so shy, she hates the public eye. I'm sorry. Are you sure you don't want to stand? Sweetie-pie, for me? On your birthday? All right. Back to Bonhoeffer. *I tried*.

Bonhoeffer was born into an amazing family. His father was the most famous psychiatrist in Germany. This was an important and an amazing family. At age fourteen he announced that he wanted to be a theologian. He got his doctorate at age twenty-one! Did anybody here get their doctorate at twenty-one? *No?* Me either. Although I just began working a week ago toward my *honorary* doctorate. Thank you. Ridiculous.

Bonhoeffer was a great theologian, but he decided in the midst of being a great theologian that he wanted to get ordained as a Lutheran pastor. And then one day at age twenty-four, he went to America to spend a year in New York City, where I live with my wife and daughter. And he went to study at Union Theological Seminary. But one Sunday a fellow student named Frank Fisher, an African American from Alabama, invited Dietrich Bonhoeffer to Harlem, to a church called Abyssinian Baptist Church.

And Bonhoeffer went with him, and for perhaps the first time in his life, in that church, he saw something that was clearly not mere *religion*. He saw people worshiping a living God. He saw people

---

she wasn't my wife and would get the joke. The only problem was that my dumb joke hinged on getting Nancy Pelosi to participate. I doubt the former Speaker of the House is accustomed to being used as a prop in the comedy routine of new acquaintances, so when I said to her *sotto voce* before I went to the podium that she should pretend to be my wife when I gestured to her, she obviously thought that I was kidding. Or she didn't quite understand. So when the great comedy moment arrived, and I gestured to her, she just smiled back at me, and the joke fell flat. Alas! Most people either assumed that the woman seated next to her (in fact, the wife of Arkansas senator Mark Pryor, who introduced me) was my wife, or were simply confused by the whole thing. I got many e-mails saying how lovely my wife looked, but the folks who sent these e-mails couldn't possibly have seen my wife, since the camera only panned to Mrs. Pryor and Nancy Pelosi. Oh, the hilarity.

Dietrich Bonhoeffer

who understood suffering and whose worship was real. Bonhoeffer said that in New York, in America, he did not hear the gospel proclaimed. Think of this! He visited many, many churches. But he did not hear the gospel proclaimed except—in his words—"in the Negro churches." That was the only place he saw the true gospel, the only place that he saw true faith, living faith. That he saw people actually living it. Preaching the gospel of Jesus. *Living* the gospel of Jesus. He saw this among the suffering in Harlem, and it changed his life.

When he got back to Germany, people could see that he was different. He wasn't intellectually different. But his heart had been changed. He began to speak publicly about the Bible as the Word of God. The living Word of God through which God who was alive wishes to speak to us. So he understood from the black church in Harlem, the idea of a personal faith that God is alive and wishes to speak to us.

Of course, it had a political component, because now it was 1931. The Nazis were rising. Bonhoeffer now began to say things that you would not hear in Germany, even in the churches in those days. He spoke of Jesus as "the man for others." He said that "whoever does not stand up for the Jews, has no right to sing Gregorian Chants!" God is not fooled!

His whole life was about this idea. That you have to have a living relationship with God and *that it must lead you to action*. That you must *obey* God. That your life will be changed, and you will somehow be different than you were before you encountered God.

Now, of course, dead religion demonizes others. I just said that. And apart from God's intervention, that is what we do. So don't think you won't do that. You *will* do that. We are broken, fallen, human beings. Apart from God, that is what we do.

We can't think that we are better than the Germans. Do you think you are better than the Germans in that era? You are not. Not in God's eyes, you are not. We are the same. We are capable of the same horrible things.

Wilberforce, somehow, saw what the people in his day didn't see, and we celebrate him for it. Bonhoeffer saw what others did not see, and we celebrate him for it.

Now how did they see what they saw? There is just one word that will answer that. It is *Jesus*. He opens our eyes to his ideas, which are different from our own, which are radical.

Now personally I would say the same thing about the unborn, that apart from God, we cannot see that they are persons as well. So those of us who know the unborn to be human beings are commanded by God to love those who do not yet see that.

We need to know that apart from God, we would be on the other side of that divide, fighting for what we believe is right. We cannot demonize our enemies. Today if you believe abortion is wrong, you must treat those on the other side with the love of Jesus.

Today, if you have a biblical view of sexuality, you will be demonized by those on the other side, who will call you a bigot. Jesus commands us to love those who call us bigots. To show them the love of Jesus. If you want people to treat you with dignity, treat *them* with dignity.

So finally, Jesus tells us that we must love our enemies. That, my friends, is the real difference between dead religion and a living faith in the God of the Scriptures, whether we can love our enemies.

Wilberforce had political enemies, but he knew that God had commanded him to treat them with civility. He knew that he had been saved by grace. He knew that he was not morally superior to the people on the other side of the aisle.

Martin Luther King told the people on the buses that you must not fight back. You must be willing to turn the other cheek—or get off the bus. Branch Rickey told Jackie Robinson, if you want to win the battle, you must do as Jesus commanded and be strong enough to *not* fight back. That is how your enemies will know that there is Someone—capital S—standing behind you. That it is not just you.

So if you can see Jesus in your enemy—in your enemy—then you can know that you are seeing with God's eyes and not your own. So can you love your enemy? If you cannot pray for those on the other side—if you cannot actually feel the love of God for your enemies, political and otherwise—my friends, that is a sure sign that you are being merely religious. That you have bought into a moral system, but you do not know the God who has forgiven you.

Only God can give us that supernatural *agape* love for those with whom we disagree. That is the test. It is an impossible standard, apart from the grace of God. We all fail that test. But thank God for the grace of God. The grace of God is real. God wants to shed it abroad in every heart. Not just on some. On *every* heart. It is the only thing—the grace of the living God—that can bring left and right together to do the right thing.

So can we humble ourselves enough to actually ask him in a real prayer to show himself to us. To lead us to do what is right? Can we do that for our country, for the world? This is a Bonhoeffer moment. If we will humble ourselves, if we ask God, if we cry out—*Cri de Couer!* Cry from the heart!—"Lord lead us!" Will you ask him to help you? The amazing grace of God. The amazing grace of God is there for everyone.

You know Jesus is not just for so-called Christians. Jesus is for everyone. For everyone. The grace of God is for everyone. I hope you know that.

———

When I was twenty-one years old, I worked at the Boston Opera House, and one day Garrison Keillor was there. He put on his show, and near the end of it he asked the audience if they wanted to sing. They didn't. But he made them anyway. He led them in a song called "Amazing Grace." And that *a cappella* rendition has stuck with me my whole life, and I thought maybe someday I will get some people to do that. Not today, of course.

But then I thought, you know, if the president can sing Al Green . . . * Then maybe you can sing with him. So we are going to try this. If it goes well, I will leave with my head up.

Are you ready? If you don't know the lyrics, pretend that you do. I want to hear harmonies:

> *Amazing Grace how sweet the sound.*
> *That saved a wretch like me.*
> *I once was lost but now I am found.*
> *Was blind, but now I see.*

God bless you.

———

* A few weeks before the prayer breakfast, the president had famously sung a few bars of a song by the famous R&B singer, Al Green.

With appreciation to Rick Potter of Potter Photo Studios for permission to

Dick Avedon, eat your heart out. History is made at the click of a shutter as the sitting US vice president takes a blurry iPhone photo of a sitting US president and the proud author whose book he solemnly promised to read.

No pressure.

(inset) This grainy photograph is perhaps the closest any of us will ever come to seeing the world through Joe Biden's eyes. Please note that there isn't a single Camaro to be seen anywhere. Hey, look! That's Nancy Pelosi hovering over the president's right shoulder!

3

CAN I GET

A PICTURE?

eople have often asked me if I was nervous while I was speaking and I can honestly say that I wasn't. On the one hand, I had been champing at the bit to get up there and get it over with, and on the other, I really was sure that the Lord was with me, which helps, in case you are wondering. My first joke fell pretty flat. I often say, "If you're here today, would you mind raising your hand. . . ." and it usually gets a big laugh. But this crowd wasn't expecting humor and most of them had no idea who I was. It would take a few minutes before they seemed to give themselves permission to laugh.

What I was thinking during the nearly thirty minutes of my speech is hard to sum up. But at the core of it all was the idea that God had arranged for me to speak to an important group of people, and most specifically, to the president of the United States and the first lady. I did not take this lightly. To allow God to speak through us is perhaps the most important thing we can ever do, so for me this was all much more than a speech. It was a holy privilege. There was almost nothing calculated about it. I wanted more than anything else to know that God's anointing was on me to say what he wanted to say for his eternal purposes. Anything else was flesh and dross and dung and worse.

I wasn't sure whether I would have the guts to hand the president my books, nor whether I would be able to publicly joke with Nancy Pelosi, nor whether I would be able to lead the crowd in singing a chorus of "Amazing Grace" at the end. These things were in God's hands.

When it was all over, I immediately went to my seat, shaking the vice president's hand as I passed. And just as I was doing so, I wondered whether it might be rude not to have gone over to the president at this point, so I asked the vice president—figuring he would know these issues of presidential protocol better than anyone—and he said yes, that I should, so I went over and greeted the president and first lady before returning to my seat.

The president spoke next, and in my soporific stupor I tried to listen as carefully as I could, wondering what it would be like to be the president of the United States, who had to be at events like this almost every single day and who had to read so many speeches that others had written for him to say. It must all seem like a terribly dull chore.

When the event was over, the president and first lady stood to leave, and again everyone else in the room—all thirty-five hundred of us—stood up as well. All you could do at this point was stand and stare at the president. There was really nothing else to be done. But rather than simply turn and leave, the president suddenly elected to go all the way to the other side of the long dais and say good-bye to each person. It was like a receiving line, except the line stays fixed and the dignitaries move along from person to person. So now the thirty-five hundred people in the room, who were standing to watch the president leave, were awkwardly frozen in place, forced to remain standing and watch the president move along the line and shake every hand. And this was happening too far away from most of them for it to be at all entertaining.

Finally the president neared me. I realized no one had taken any photos of us together, and this would be the only opportunity in which to get a photo with him. So I pulled out my iPhone and got it ready. I asked the vice president if he thought I would be able to get a photo with the president. "Oh, sure!" he said, in that hearty way he has. "I'll get that for you." Meaning that he would snap the picture of the two of us. But I really couldn't imagine allowing the vice president of the United States to suffer the mild indignity of taking a photo of the president and me! That was asking far too much. But suddenly the president was upon us. He shook my hand.

"I'm going to read your book!" he said.

"Can I get a picture?" I asked.

"Sure!"

I was just about to turn and snap the photo of the two of us myself, as I had done earlier with Nancy Pelosi, but Vice President Biden wouldn't stand for it. "Here, let me do that," he said, in what was a distinctly avuncular tone. The vice president of the United States now took my iPhone and snapped a picture of President Obama and me. It was a very gracious thing for him to do. Not only do I have the photographic proof of this in the actual photo of the president and me, but I also have photographic proof in that the official White House photographer was there to take a picture of the vice president taking our picture! It was all too much. And if this wasn't enough, the thirty-five hundred who were pinned like beetles, standing and watching all this, witnessed the moment. It seemed historical somehow. A vice president taking a photo of a president. One can only imagine Spiro Agnew taking a Polaroid shot of Nixon. Or the impeachable Vice President Andrew Johnson muscling Matthew Brady away from his tripod to snap a sepia-toned image of President Lincoln!

But there was still one more memorable moment before the president and first lady vanished from all of us. As the Obamas now waved to the crowd and made their final—we thought—exit upstage, people in the crowd noticed that they had left their two signed Metaxas biographies on the dais, right next to their breakfast plates. It's a funny thing, but almost everyone in that room had their eyes fixed on the president, and most of them seemed to be aware that he was leaving the two books behind. It was a great drama unfolding. Would he really leave them behind? But happily, some bright presidential aide must have noticed the same thing and told the president, just before he stepped behind the curtains and out of view, because suddenly, with everyone standing and watching this drama, he now turned around and walked all the way back to the front of the stage, where he had been sitting, and retrieved the books. The whole crowd almost cheered this unscripted and extraordinary moment!

And then he was gone. And just as suddenly as he was out of everyone's sight, the pressure seemed to be let out of the room. Everyone was free to sit and talk. Everyone wanted to talk, but who wanted to sit? People now could find their friends or roam toward the exits. For my part, I had no idea what to do. I wanted to talk to my friends and family. Suddenly they appeared not far from me, but separated from the stage by a barrier. And in a few more minutes they were able to come up onto the stage, where we hugged and talked and took pictures, basking in the glow of whatever had just happened for as long as we would be permitted to do so.

These moments with my wife and daughter and my mother and father and aunt and uncle and a few of our dearest friends were extremely special. Joel Tucciarone had come down from New York. Gordon Pennington had flown in from Michigan; Martha Linder had flown up from Lakeland, Florida. Jim Lane and his wife, Susie, and B. J. Weber and his wife, Sheila, were there. I was exhausted, and I was blessed, and I was glad it was over. What had happened? Had I imagined it all? Who can fathom such things? What do we say about them?

Praise the Lord.

Proudly introducing my wife and daughter (in the blurry right foreground) to the man who is one heartbeat away from the presidency. To my left are Senator Mark Pryor and his wife. Did I mention that this took place on my wife's 39th birthday? For those tuning in late, Nancy Pelosi is not my wife.

———•———

(below) With my mom onstage, just after the breakfast. Behind us are my dear friends Jim Lane and Martha Linder. Having my friends and family with me on this extraordinary day was certainly the biggest blessing of all.

With appreciation to Rick Potter of Potter Photo Studios for permission to use (both photos)

WATCH THE ADDRESS

The National Prayer Breakfast has graciously
made a video of the speech available.
Follow the link here and enjoy:

www.nelsonfree.com/deadreligion

ABOUT THE AUTHOR

Eric Metaxas grew up in Danbury, Connecticut, and graduated from Yale University in 1984. He is the author of the New York Times bestsellers *Bonhoeffer: Pastor, Martyr, Prophet, Spy* and *Amazing Grace: William Wilberforce and the Heroic Campaign to End Slavery*. His writing has appeared in the *New York Times*, *Washington Post*, and the *Atlantic Monthly*, and he has appeared as a cultural commentator on CNN and Fox News. He is the founder and host of Socrates in the City, the acclaimed Manhattan speakers' series on "life, God, and other small topics." Eric lives in New York City with his wife and daughter.

Subscribe to Eric's e-mail newsletter at ERICMETAXAS.COM
Follow Eric at Twitter: @ericmetaxas

ALSO FROM ERIC METAXAS

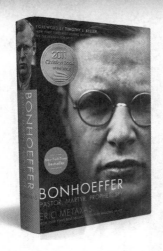

A definitive, deeply moving narrative, Bonhoeffer is a story of moral courage in the face of the monstrous evil that was Nazism. After discovering the fire of true faith in a Harlem church, Bonhoeffer returned to Germany and became one of the first to speak out against Hitler. As a double-agent, he joined the plot to assassinate the Führer, and was hanged in Flossenberg concentration camp at age 39. Since his death, Bonhoeffer has grown to be one of the most fascinating, complex figures of the 20th century.

"Insightful and illuminating, this tome makes a powerful contribution to biography, history and theology."

—PUBLISHERS WEEKLY

"[A] massive and masterful new biography."

—CHRISTIANITY TODAY

"Metaxas tells Bonhoeffer's story with passion and theological sophistication."

—WALL STREET JOURNAL

Available wherever books and ebooks are sold

In *Seven Men, New York Times* best-selling author Eric Metaxas presents seven exquisitely crafted short portraits of widely known—but not well understood—Christian men, each of whom uniquely showcases a commitment to live by certain virtues in the truth of the gospel.

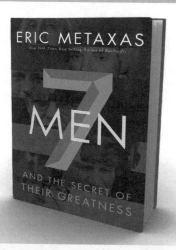

Written in a beautiful and engaging style, *Seven Men* addresses what it means (or should mean) to be a man today, at a time when media and popular culture present images of masculinity that are not the picture presented in Scripture and historic civil life. What does it take to be a true exemplar as a father, brother, husband, leader, coach, counselor, change agent, and wise man? What does it mean to stand for honesty, courage, and charity, especially at times when the culture and the world run counter to those values?

Each of the seven biographies represents the life of a man who experienced the struggles and challenges to be strong in the face of forces and circumstances that would have destroyed the resolve of lesser men. Each of the seven men profiled—George Washington, William Wilberforce, Eric Liddell, Dietrich Bonhoeffer, Jackie Robinson, John Paul II, and Charles Colson—call the reader to a more elevated walk and lifestyle, one that embodies the gospel in the world around us.

THOMAS NELSON
Since 1798